Matters of Reality: Body, Mind, and Soul

C. Liegh McInnis

Psychedelic Literature/Jackson, Mississippi

Psychedelic Literature ®

203 Lynn Lane
Clinton, MS 39056
(601) 383-0024
psychedeliclit@bellsouth.net

Copyright © 1996, 2007 by C. Liegh McInnis for Psychedelic Literature. All Rights Reserved, including the right of reproduction in whole or in part in any form without permission in writing from the author.

LCCN: 96-092620
ISBN: (13 digit) 978-0-9655775-7-1
ISBN: (10 digit) 0-9655775-7-0

Other Works by C. Liegh McInnis
The Lyrics of Prince (Lyrical Criticism, 1997)
Scripts: Sketches and Tales of Urban MS (Fiction, 1998)
Confessions: Brainstormin' from Midnight 'til Dawn (Poetry, 1998)
Searchin' for Psychedelica (Poetry, 1999)
Prose: Essays and Letters (Social Commentary, 1999)
Da Black Book of Linguistic Liberation (Poetry, 2002)
Poetic Discussions (Interviews, DVD 2005)
Introduction of a Blues Poet (Poetry, CD 2005)

Acknowledgements

To God, the Supreme Creator, it's been a gloriosofantastic ride. Hallowed by Thy name.

To Monica, my female image, (Soul of my Soul), your love, strength, patience, and comfort keep me going. [i] love you.

To Jeff Gibson, one day our Black Room of Poets Anthology will come to life. "[i] promise you."

To my father, Claude Sr., [i] hope that you can see that [i] was listening. The knowledge and wisdom has been invaluable. Thanks and love.

To my mother, Claudette W., you are the most beautiful and intelligent person [i] have ever known. [i] have no greater respect for anyone. Thanks for a wonderful life.

To Rosalie Winfield (Grandmamma), you're the best.

To Rosalie Winfield, Jr. (Li'l Rosie), thanks for brightening my light.

To Imogene Morgan, thanks for the love

To Iola Fisher, you told us we could be anything.

To Curtis McInnis, this is as real as it gets. Thanks.

To Mr. Wilbert and Bonnie Gardner, none of this would have been possible without you.

To Dr. Walter M. Hurns, [i] know that you know but thanks for everything.

To Dr. Marie O'Banner Jackson, you listened when [i] wanted to whine. Your wisdom has carried me.

To George Fisher (G. Fish), your music is an inspiration. [i] often hear your funk when [i] write.

To John Fisher, that hook in "Fever for Yo' Love Tonight" is too funky. Your support has helped me along the way.

To Ricki Graham, for all of those talks under the cover of the moonlight. You listened and understood. Thanks.

To Eric Clowers, a good friend, thanks for the support.

To the Jackson State University English Department, thanks for the tolerance and nurturing.

To the community of Clarksdale, Mississippi, thanks for planting seeds and watering my growth.

And to P, thanks for striving to be all that you could. Because of that, a young kid from the Mississippi Delta was able to dream and achieve. You are the reason [i] became a writer. Peace and Be Wild.

p.s. This is for all the funky people who just wanna be themselves. Life ain't nothing but a gathering of souls. Let's start sharing each other's energy instead of burning each other out. Peace to West Jackson.

Table of Contents

Foreword	6
Welcome to the Dawn	8
Greetings	10
Journey de la Intuitive	11
Lost: Looking for the Dawn	13
The Black Room of Poets	15
Soft as Evening Rain	17
[i] Want to Know Why: It Ain't Existential Is It?	18
My Blooze for You	19
Black Angel	22
Get All the Love Your Heart Can Hold	23
"Bang!"	25
---Just a Thought of Mankind…?	26
Afrianna	28
[i] Long to Touch Infinity	30
Indigo Jazz	31
Mental Anguish	32
Connection	34
Traces of Old Lovers	35
Your Money's Life	37
She Became My Soul	39
…written for strong sistas such as you	40
Fever for Yo' Love Tonight	42
A Matter of the Dissolution of the Ghetto	44
The Evil of Integration	46
Vote!	49
A Bullet for the Drug Dealer	50
Black In…	51
…speaking from Masculine to Feminine	53
Corner-Stone	55
Mother of Illegitimates	57
The Ramblings of a Scarred Mind	58
Of Reality and Perception	60
StarGazer	61
Is There a Difference Between Purple and Grape?	62
Time	63
Another Trip on the Eve of Insanity	65
Silent Conscience	67
Children of Trouble	69
Pop Poetry	70
Afterword	71

(Foreword) To Whom It May Concern:

If your heart is as crystal clear as sun-blown glass, if there is a traveling fire in your soul, and if you possess an autonomous ocean for a mind, then the gray hazed windows of your perception may about to be windexed to reveal a New Year's Eve of a time. If you are absent or prodigal from all of these, then [i] suggest you close this collection now. [i] declare not these expressions to be the gospels of anything. They are, however, the attempts of a writer to try and get at what he is through a mosaic of the memory and the now, slowly marinated with saucy honesty, basted with buttered reflection, churned and amalgamated into pressed leaves, yet devoid of training wheels. (Falling is to walking as broken shells are to omelets, and pain is to knowing as night is to day. You can't transcend the smoke until you know how hot Hell is.)

If your Canterbury heart is looking for (T)ruth or salvation, [i] suggest you look under the preacher's robe. These are points of view that don't necessarily stick as wallpaper to centered cultural certainties. It is in this sense of a writer, a shepherd, that [i] never wish to attempt to be. For poets, like their slippery sloped words, are cinnamon liars, carnival mirrors, one-eyed prophets, pack rats of history, car salesmen of sundry fates, and makers of none. With this work, it is only for the reader and time to take what one will either as gas for their car, or manure for their fields, or simply to mark a notch in the wall of time, like old pictures of people whom we don't know. This is poetry where moments are thumbnails in the deck of cards of our lives, a road trip where my Aristotlilian photographs form a busy intersection with the flickering realm of my fragmented Freudian existence, just that moment before we are certain of which shoe goes on which foot. Of course, perception is reality because rainy days register differently depending on what you have planned or what you are wearing.

Experience what you will, censor as you feel, and condemn what you must. But go. Allow yourself to be driven in the car of somebody else's imagination down the highway of their reality. Understanding is the yeast to knowing. Like it or not, all of our interstates cross at the intersection of the same Parade, even if we are reading different maps.

Sincerely,
C. Liegh

Welcome to the Dawn

...and again bloody Light was pulled screaming from the belly of Darkness. There was an august rumbling through the pregnant Universe as it expanded and returned again in on itself like a great chest inhaling and exhaling in a fertilizing manner. Chalky Constellations against the night's blackboard realigned themselves in the eruption of seven. Pandemonium, race riots in reverse, explodes violently into clam—the parturition process. Green showers washed away soiled brown rings of history...as the nymph child in high heels spoke.

And God looked down upon his flock, ejaculated down his aesthetic omnipotence, giving birth to the poet. One whose ears cradle His words like a baby's mama when the iron ears of society are deaf from the constant clang of aluminum hearts banging against steel actions. One who's able to read "dehumanization" when it's mis-spelled and mis-pronounced "civil-lie-zation." One who, like penguins returning home to give birth, looks to Nature and finds our umbilical chord that leads back to the Garden. The poet is a blood bridge between man and his Womb. Eshu is the echo of His vibrating voice that rattles us into movement like a bass, centering us on the one. Can you find middle C?

Welcome to the Dawn.
You may leave your tattered physical
that hangs off you like soaked wash rags at the
exit doors of your faded reality.
Keep your body (a dented, scratched, and stalling jalopy)
bloated and pilling from the acid of selfishness;
[i] want your underdeveloped mind
to squish and drip through my words like liquid clay.
[i] shall provide a feast of well seasoned words
on which your famished soul shall dine.
Poetry is the jazzy wake of your first life,
the erupting orange Dawn of your second.
Let go your vicious and venomous viper fears, which

encase you in a concrete cage of social anxieties,
keeping you from soul-shaking hands
with your authentic psyche.
Let go your heavy luggage of guilt
that sags you into nothingness.
Charity is the only Law.
It hath benevolence and a rod
that cannot be vetoed or bent by any government.
And let go your flaming embarrassment.
Love hath no silly shame
and individuals no landloving judge.
For our genuine birthright is to Baldwin each other.
Imprisonment is not an act of rehabilitation,
for Plato's world of "tangible things" is but a jail cell.
The soul, like summer sunlight,
is too bold for any man to hold.
Yes,…welcome to the Dawn where individuals
become rushing rivers flowing freely into the Sun.

Greetings

From the shallow pits of God's Black stomach,
orange and yellows and reds and greens
swirl like melted chocolates into
a juicy center of creation.
Now, is your mind erect?

What's up? Are you an empty or a full cup?
Does your sandpaper dry throat thirst for more
than the literary scientists in their pale walls
have given you before?
(Tired of counting form that equates to your invisibility?)
Has your mind's cherry been popped?
By the time Electra's clock chimes
hopefully we, together, stuck like peanut butter and jelly,
will find and clean the CIA spaces in the
back closet of your jumbled mind,
that's been infected with the virus of normality.
[i]'m so glad you decided to be watered.
There are so many moving muses
who would like to place misty kisses
inside your mind…
But, remember that
there are narcotic nymphs who are loose liars
as well as fairies who are frighteningly factual,
and if you begin to feel that
your reality has been placed into a blender,
maybe it's a figurative snapshot
from my cubed fiction that you must steal
to eye-dentify and deal.
But at all times deduct from the ATM of your mind
the currency needed to purchase your desired reality.
For anyone else's reality for you
is more than likely an upside down truth,
or a lie in a new shiny suit.

So dig up, [i]'m gonna teach you a new trick.
Or, at least, give you some mo' colors fo' yo' brush.

Journey de la Intuitive

There is a locomotive on the left side of my brain,
and it leaves port to places not yet drawn on our maps,
carrying passengers to a rainbow of destinations
of their syncopated red organ
that drums the song of their lives,
composing a minuet that leads to a Yellow Day
and of seven forever they be a part.

Under the golden flaked
just above flowing fuchsia meadow,
a wind blows and bounds into a rolling wave.
(Sight bends in on itself at the dips in the wave.
Single vision is spun into purple possibilities.)
A cloying and creamy road to revelation is carved,
and with clovers of diamonds it is paved.
This wave is a cheetah racing the wind, ears lain back
with a desire to touch and taste everything twice,
blowing them into Euphoria.
Feel pink sensations as she brushes
silk softly against your inners.

This orgasmic blueberry is before
words stiffen into concrete.
This Jacob's jigsaw is before the theory wilts in calculation.
This sovereign and shapeless liquid is before the soul has
been poured into the rigid, cold container of normality.
Here is where the stem of your actions
pollinates the bud of your dreams.
Here is where the single cell of "what you are"
divides into the organism of "who you wish to be."
And the "Be" verb is a running river
rather than a bed of fossils.
Here is the tree free from the impotent sign
and the "thought" in its unfallen, pre-apple purity.

This is the odyssey between mind and mouth.

There are ideas in their wedding gown innocence.

There are intentions free from greenback ambitions.
Allow the silvery shine of the sublime to bathe you
before we dull it with a sallow sign.
They are all here in their infant glory,
here in your gray dome before
being encased in paralyzing phonemes
weighted with the baggage of gangrene greed.

Enjoy, for tomorrow the idea becomes petrified
in the mind's museum,
and reality becomes the coward who breeds the notion
that the road to Hell is paved with good intentions.
Yet, [i] believe that road is paved with the
business of the church and the politics of religion,
which then enslaves big bang thought
under the false flag of a reversed cross,
the bloody sign of shackled dreams and broken hopes
(The sadness of language is that it cries
when moneychangers molest it, infecting the people
with culturally diseased ideas.)

Do your words open or close, unlock or lock doors?
Which way is your key turning?
Does your brain need some fiber?

Lost: Looking for the Dawn

Looking for the Dawn with a map edited by a lobbyist,
designed to keep Bigger on the circular path of a redundant
interstate so that he never finds the strawberry suburbia of
integration's pie, the wooly haired boy loses his way
on the bypass of inverted religion.
So, the brother bought a gun as a supplement to his faith.
The paled Angel of Hate told him it was the only
legislation to feed his soul's sunken stomach in a city
polluted with political phalli.
Tricked him into looking to his Mandingo mythology
for his salvation and restoration.
None of his days were yellow.
So he began to sleep with the color green.
No sunshine on his eroding body,
like tulips in a pawn shop,
the little brother withered like winter roses.
His body never had communion with his soul.
The rotted algae of Hate became his conscience,
as he bathes in the mucus white light of Hell's Earth.
Another cracked voice joins the choir,
the noise of crows in a Kroger sack deafens them to
the fluid flutes of serenity.

Now gun shots ring like lullabies to insane souls.

Bullets sprout from a pus-filled open sore of pain,
growing like a fungus of anger
that explodes through the barrel of his steeled magnum.

Working in a blind fold, playing pin the tale on the Negro,
never knowing he is the Negro pinning his own ass,
little brother can't find the Dawn by his molested map.
Sucking, snorting, and smoking
his glass and powder pacifiers,
artificial highs never get you off the ground.
His borrowed map leads him, like a drugged rat in a dead-
end maze, to a destination that others have chosen for him.

Pop fixes fill his little bag of tricks.
Skinning and grinning like a Clarence running for
impotent office, he integrates into an empty school.
Humping 'til four in the morning,
his dry seeds evaporate like his faint ideas.
Looking deep into his mind's cracked mirror,
double blank stares interrupt his slumber;
he's a king without a throne,
a Mr. Rogers without a neighborhood,
constantly reading the wrong book for the test.

The Black Room of Poets

Four-cornered Blackness, a cubed onyx of power,
a swollen pen erect and pulsating
with electric anxiety like inmates longing for their lovers,
or rivers longing to be reunited with oceans.
The souls of budding Black flowers
appear as charcoal gray silhouettes
against the leafy fabric of ancestral bibliographies.
The night shakes like a tambourine and beats
like a tom-tom vibrating across the watery cosmos,
merging and returning like God's promise to Himself.
This bright Black glow which covers the room expands like
a filling belly as each feed upon
the caramel ideas of the other.
"This is my mind;
partake of Africa's Harlem communion."
Deer quick and Christmas-light bright waves flash against
the marble walls of soil rich brain chambers producing a
well-plotted tradition where vernacular is the tool that
carves a road back to Langston's dusty rivers.
[i] build; therefore, [i] am.
[i] language; therefore, [i] continue.

Thoughts grow limber, rubbery appendages
and become Ideas.
Ideas grow muscular arms and legs
and become Visions.
Visions endure puberty and become Concepts
that bookmark our time in History's Broadway production.
Together, it's a metaphysical anthology
read by eyes with no face.
Off Black and soft Black and light Black and dark Black
(hair and sky and coals and skin)
crash up against each other like words
hurled around in a philosophic car crash,
blending like mixed drinks, revising themselves,
becoming elastic solids and then dissolving like
salt into water becoming burnt offerings.
It's the constant shedding of skin of Black phraseology,

a flowing stream of lives etched out
by pictorial locution.

Midnight burns into the Dawn
as Eshu keeps firm watch
while writers willingly suffer osmosis,
pieces of thought taking refuge within another,
hands continuously remolding Black clay,
pulling all of the colors of the rainbow from
the prismatic soul of the Dark poet,
who becomes a Black smudge
on the white lie of canonization,
sprinkling polychromatic phrases on the page
like fine brown sugar creatin' a new breed of bakers.
Funk fo' yo' soul—
"Reproduction of the New Breed"
sprouts from the loins of ancient bards,
the Black light radiates, shining a beacon for
the next group of sailors
over the vast ocean of Black words.

Soft as Evening Rain

Simply, as [i] lie upon my bed of green,
a swaying, race-car curved flutter of emotions
rush like stampeding stallions through my head,
freely shifting my center of thought
like leaves in a fall breeze,
sending flashing memories of summer passion
dancing their tickling small feet over my volcanic body
as an orchestra of tears plays me a wild symphony.
    When [i]'m with you a confetti of sharp emotions
    from throbbing crimson to crying blue
    slice through me like sunshine through ice.
    When you smile a warm blanket of calm covers me.
        It's like kissing with emotions
        soft as evening rain.

Your lemon flavored rain sliding slowly against my soul,
it's a Ferris wheel ride where [i] never see the ground,
and joy converges on itself like a never-ending horizon.
It's a strawberry balloon that explodes
pop rocks on the tip of my tongue.
Kiwi scented rain comes up from beneath our conversation
and dances a jig on the cheesecake sidewalk.
    Now [i] lay with my ancient anticipation
    hoping for some type of liquid emancipation.

        Camped out on the hill is the Dawn.
        Just behind her is the Sun,
        as Music kisses us lightly,
        putting me to sleep soft as evening rain.

[i] Want to Know Why: It Ain't Existential, Is It?

[i] announced to the scraping sky tree, "Sir, [i] exist."
Its branches and leaves continued stoically
to defy gravity holding statue still.
[i] announced to the businessman ant, "Sir, [i] exist,"
and he continued his blue-collar march over my foot.

[i] looked deep into the sky
as far as my eyes could take me
beyond the cotton clouds,
and [i] only saw blue inside of itself.
No winged answers fell from the great beyond.
It began to rain…[i] never saw it coming.

[i] walked; my heart did its mathematical thing.
[i] ran; it played a Saturday night sax solo.
Salty sweat began to ooze and trickle
down my prickling arms, legs, and spine.
[i] finally felt that [i] was swelling with life.
[i] was only feeling faint from having run to fast.

My mind, like a worn rubber, grows weary
of "[i] think; therefore, [i] am."
[i] want to know why.
How and What are sterile scientific calculations
devoid of von Schiller's "Human Knowledge."
Cause even after hours of
coma inducing sex, [i] am still empty of why.

> "Nobody loves me but my mother,
> and she could be jivin' to."
> from *Indianola Mississippi Seeds*
>
> B. B. King

My Blooze for You

Mornin' cum when it want to baby,
but not fo' de nite have its way wit'chu.
and jus' when you think dat my good times 'bout to start
da wind with da bill collector's scent tells me dat its thru.

You's a evil no good demon, baby,
who can make it alrite in fifteen minutes.
You make me feel like [i]'m da main when you want me to,
then like a li'l boy when you thru.

All my life been outside, lookin' fo' a way to get in,
but every answer [i] gave life was marked wrong,
[i] must be whiter than Adam's original sin.
Love wuz a transvestite to me, baby,
de only female [i] knew wit'a dick.
Cried a river of eternity when [i] realized
dat makin' my money disappear is yo' best trick.
And you wonder why [i] do de thangs dat [i] do.
It's 'cause [i]'m baptized in my blooze fo' you.

Da sun done set on another day.
Guess dis jingle dey gimme
is s'posed to be a workin' day's pay.
But [i] don't see how [i] works thirty days,
and dey gets half my pay.

Back doh slamin' when [i] open da front,
must be da middle of de month.
Say you can't depend on me no mo';
so, you open yo' legs like a liquor store.
Say you got to make yo'self a way
'til [i] meet my next pay day.

Draggin' home wit'da loose coins in my hand
da house smell like you been wit' two, three men.
Another man on da down stroke,
playin' house wit'me is a big ass joke.
[i] hope he left her some money on da table
'cause we sho' nuff broke.

        But dems da blooze,
        sandpaper times and shady news,
        troubles coming in twos.
        When you need lay-away to pay dues,
        dems da blooze.

Sunshine ain't nuthin' but heat
beatin' down on my face,
remindin' an ugly ducklin' like me
to keep in my "low rent love" place.

Rain ain't nuthin' but tears,
not washin' but makin' my pain mo' severe,
and you stand yo' pretty ass there
wonderin' what's wrong,
tryin' to decide where on Earth
has dat gentle man gone.
Well, [i]'m standin' rite here,
pourin' out de ugly truth.
All of my crippled up and broke down actions
like a river run rite back to my blooze fo' you.

My scarred, rough hands scratch
yo' silk soft face.
My body is gravel, and yours is lace.
To even dream of havin' you
is like beatin' a man holdin' a fifth ace,
and the family of voices in my head
keep remindin' me of my fungi growin' faults.
Wishin' [i] was dead becomes my only thought.

Lovin' you is too much to go thru,

[i]'m a junkie strung out on my blooze fo' you.

Don't truly kno' how to love.
[i]'m an elephant more than a dove.
[i]'m a bull in a china shop,
[i]'m a man with somewhere to be who ain't go no watch.
So de next time you axe why [i] do de crazy shit dat [i] do,
it be because of my blooze fo' you.

Black Angel

Midnight bright, a blazing fire of night,
you float from the clouds puffed full of onyx.
Glowing, you shine, moonlight dancing
and your before the ancient history image
slides like chiffon across my receptive skin,
making me know that Hallelujahs
can be found in the splashes of your kisses.
Body chiseled from the dark of the sky,
lips pure as Jesus' grape nectar,
your loud whisper calls me to a deeper space,
within lost chambers of my heart's ear, reaffirming
that bodies don't have to be bodies forever.

Creamy, ebony lather of soap,
your skin seeps into mine,
washing me with every embrace.
Paved, blacktop diamonds, your eyes
reveal time's new covenant as your wings
weave a crystal salvation around me.
The wells of my eyes run wet for you.
When you smile, the glow of the eternal licks my body.
Spread your wings and allow me to soar in you.
Your inside Blackness shines of pearls.
Black showers of sunshine,
lighting a path to where lions play with lambs.
[i] will sacrifice myself unto you.

Get All the Love Your Heart Can Hold

[i] think that the air conditioner of her past
was blowing winter memories that day…
the goose pimples on her heart said
it was kinda chilly in there.
So [i] walked over to turn up the thermostat,
but her eyes said that [i] was pushin' the wrong button.
As [i] went swimming in her brown lenses,
all that could be seen was
a vacant room colored in pale primer.
It was haunted by a sooty shadow that
crossed the room Grim Reaper style
and entered into my heart like worms diving for food.
Without Love's furnace, a body will freeze to death.
Love, the ultimate Diehard Battery,
the body's central heating unit,
needs to be primed like a pump once and a while.

Knee-deep emotional sewage rising above my head,
[i], with no rhetorical gas mask,
thought it all better left alone.
But even buried within frigid emptiness,
her pilot light was still lit and flickered faintly
through the haze and mist of her blurry eyes.
Yet, in my scattered pieces of cerebral engagement,
[i] had found myself a roommate within
her crumbly white orbed doorless and windowless attic.
Her inner tears, icicle sharp and piranha piercing,
hooked me, embracing me in a numbing blizzard.
[i], struggling from beneath her snow storm, was a
bumbling lifeguard who may freeze with her even though
[i] felt she wanted to die like she had no friends.

But, [i], as sure as fertilizer is warm,
wasn't ready to meet Jesus,
and thinking on her hourglass soul [i] wasn't ready to
give her up as terminally frost-bitten food.

Her pilot remained though her eyes were

cemented in the flurry of past emotions.
Yet, Love, like roadside flowers belonging to no one,
appears and survives where nothing else can.
There was a whisper inside of me
that grew into a sea of fire, exploding
like a burgundy oil well, raining red and blue drops,
thawing her like trees budding in May.

Love's flame is hotter than the basement of Hell.
For Love is an emperor penguin that finds heat in the snow.
Your heart is a cup;
fill it with as much hot cider as it can hold.
You may never know when someone else needs a sip.

"Bang!"

A single shot shattering the silent night,
my thoughts grow twitching Ichabod limbs and wander,
like a creeping Crane, up the streets painted in plasma,
down the alleys perfumed in piss,
across the city with crooked byways
that zig zag to money's plastic beat
to find a corner of a space in my mind
to ask whose file has just been deleted
from our collective computer program?
This hollow is not sleepy.

[i] lie on a bed of emotional nails and wonder
whose life has been blown out like a cheap candle?
What family's sparkling dreams
have just been smashed into glass pieces?
[i] stare like a sacrificial soldier into the darkness
as the night cries thick tears across my sunken chest.
Black tears, saturated with broken promises longing to run
into its river of final rest, carry in its waters the rings of
forgotten shots that reverberate like broken speakers
against the wall of Time, vibrating in a spinning motion,
the sound smashing against my window, breathing hot
against my face.
[i] suffocate on the smell of a mass drunk on its own filth.
That slug of sound slithering into my room reminds me of
my Siamese connection to shadows outside my window.

Now [i] lay me down to sleep
with a .32 and a .38 at me feet.

> "If [i] came back as a dolphin,
> would you listen to me then?"
> from "Dolphin"

---Just a Thought of Mankind...?

The world is a board game;
would have never guessed that the mark of the beast
looks like the Kroger card.
You must choose: Day people or Night people.
The Lefties and the Righties are carving up the spaces
like a seventh dimension Berlin Conference Proclamation,
where Have is a race.
Hair must be parted and worn to the left.
Your tie must be eight inches from the bottom button,
and your color is what you sell of it.
Now you are a mirror of their ideas
lost in the soma smog of the *Brave New World*.
The Politics of Likeness where religion can be rolled
and smoked or dispensed in pills.
They are the NRICP:
The New Republic of the
Institutionalized Conformist Party,
and they are armed with the fear
of those afraid to be excluded.

But where are the recipes that [i] like to cook?
My mouth can never water for the national M.R.E.,
(Meals Ready to Eat), devoid of history's plural flavor.
Where are my psalms, my narratives, my versifications?
Does it bother you that you cannot kill
all of the cockroaches,
especially those who refuse
to be smothered by your thick gravy allegory?
Does your fear have a larger phallus than you?
Thus, none of your epics are true, not even to you,
and your manufactured society is barren
because you never realized that

James Brown is a natural resource.

But, [i]'m sorry; [i] just can't dance
to that tired ass iron rhythm without Funk for chance!

You and [i] remain as separate as the moon and the sun,
but you don't hear me tho'…
Sing "o" birds of the park,
and let 'em know that
paisley can be seen in the dark!

                              From your inbreeding of ideas,
                              an impotent world you've become.
                              An evolution of destruction,
                              DAMN, that's dumb-----------!

Afrianna

I

Afrianna winds herself around us,
stroking us with a pool of love's hot chocolate,
(Her tranquil breath blows against our face,
swooshing down our backs),
presenting us with a playful time
within the romper room of her mind.
This crystalline cherub seeks to replenish us daily.
Flowing like the Nile, her cupped hands push
the waves and ruffle the leaves.
She inhales, her breasts rounding and filling
with maya she removes from us,
her lungs spin spiritual photosynthesis,
exhaling, pushing clear chastity into our nostrils.
She is the gist of our breath.
The vanilla breeze of our autumn
and the jumbay syncopation of our hearts,
she blows us into fudge ecstasy.
Cradling us with her mattress arms,
she caresses us with her feathery fingertips.
Her lips sprinkle kisses smelling of daffodil nectar,
refreshing us to the marrow of our bones.
Hypnotic, it smothers us, drowns us
deep within the V of her vivacity.

II

If [i] allow you to strip me naked before my fears
what shall [i] gain?
If [i] let you blow me like the leaves,
where would you leave me?
Would you cause tiny mental spasms
with your breezy kisses?
Or, would you place upon my face
one of your long sweeping cherry kisses
and leave me forever transfixed like Mona Lisa's smile
in a moment of you?

Thinking of you,
dandelions race through my head,
while butterflies and salmon swim up the stream
created by your crashing against my firm fantasies,
and [i] wade in a dream that runs into the horizons of
forever.

III

Afrianna abides with us, winding herself as a
pillow of landscape beneath our heads, or
sitting like a nymph at our feet, or blowing through us
as a blazing aroma of nectarine fields and cranberry
streams.
And upon us, she rains
her honey moist wetness across our skins.
Her fingers of flowers brush across us,
cooling our electricity.
With a basket full of Nature,
she is God's Pocahontas,
taking life from flower to lung and back again.

[i] Long to Touch Infinity

No 7:30 a.m. should be the same as the last.
You have become an inmate to your daily rituals,
a mouse in the maze of bills paid and trying to get laid.
"What time is it?" plays like an eternally broken record.
Yesterday is today is the same stale slice of bread.
Yet at the edge of my mind's waters
[i] remember pyramids.
In the fourth chamber of my sleep
[i] see mapped constellations that lead me
back to a moment when [i] heard
the raspy bellow of God's vocal.
[i] need to mix colors that help me better see.
My dammed mind longs for waters
that rush to the equator of infinity.

> Dance if you want to;
> the Master's throwing a jam,
> and [i] want to be there for some
> Psychedelic Charity,
> getting high off some native, wild flower
> clarity 'cause my heart longs
> to touch infinity.

Lilac stars hang in a tequila sky.
Someone taught elephants to fly.
The clock on the wall has no hands.
This trip goes deep into "Electric Lady Land."
If this be a dream, don't let me awake.
Let's just receive all the love our hearts' cup can take.
Let's hang out the windows with no walls.
Let's take a class with no roll call.
Remember…your mind is your mind,
and your brush paints your reality.
[i] just want to know how many licks it takes
to get to the eye of infinity?

Indigo Jazz

In a box of four-cornered smoke
on a night with no name,
sits a leather faced soothsayer.
His beard, sprinkled with dashes of salt,
an annotation of miles, frames his face,
each curved line a chapter in his story.
His paintbrush fingers play
the dissertation of our lives.

His bent and ashen hands on the keys like an orator on a
tale, making his musical emotion elixir,
memories floating through the room like fog on the ocean,
every beat a moment where time exhales,
every note a different color of empathy,
every chorus a mounting scene,
every song a play written by a community of hands.
He's reading from the great book of life,
chronicling our archives,
a swaying four bar thesis, heavy on the immediate imagery.

Songs you slip on like well worn clothes,
every stitched or buttoned note
quilts the tattered patterns of the past.

Three a.m. he's playing to a room full of damp pity.
Every fool with a story is jerked, Easy Jesus style,
by the grumbling undertones of the bass.
Like sliding rain, tears streak down the mountain of your
regret hanging on a soggy cheek paralyzed by Time until
a moan in the key of pain sends it splashing to the floor,
splattering into crystal flakes of yesterday.
Picking up his discarded notes, panhandling for thoughtful
pennies, you return wounded-bird style, broken wing and
dented beak, on this same no-named night
to playback the recorder of your wrong turns,
and drink down the bitter barley of his voice.

Mental Anguish

Pain is the broken glass promises
we tried to glue with crack.
Reality stings an alcoholic truth to a liar's laceration,
like the salt of accountability to a political slug.
Absentee voices wail like banshees
all the way to the bone of my repository.
Visions run together like road-kill stew,
blurring and blasting reversed eyes into glossy sight
where hands are hidden in the dark of fear…

… is this the place?

Insanity is a home remedy that dulls the pain.
Or, is the prescription's impotence and nausea
more disturbing than living in an upside down world?

My head's muscle throbs of too many pushups.
Reality is a gut stuffed into pants two sizes too small.
Reality is a movie with more scenes than my mind has film,
converging constantly on themselves like sand,
swiftly sliding downhill into a hole filling rapidly,
covering the skeletal ideas of whom [i] used to be.
Now a prisoner of my own pint-sized proclamations,
boxed in by barren lines drawn in the dirt of boundaries,
trapped in the smelly pits of my imagination,
smiled at by teeth with no mouth.

Yet, Insanity is the only cherub willing to make a deal
for my washed-out wits if [i] but trade in my will
like old furniture.
My mind thinks itself free
like a slave on a path to nowhereville,
longing to be someone other than my jack-in-the-box,
pulling chained strings, lowering the fragile draw bridge
of my mind's fourth dimension, where wet ghosts curse the
darkness, hell hounds bark in a sample loop, and a dj
cutting with knives a song that only has a middle.
[i] drink bleach to erase the taste

of dried crazy on my tongue;
[i] stab pencils into my swelling eardrum,
to rewrite the dialogue of the play in my head,
while the horny devil and the church folks
cast lots for my soul.

Truth hides in a muddy maze of slippery lies
fertilized by man's need for cherry flavored religion.
Salvation is a work of art dat [i] hang in my family room.
Death is the mattress
that awaits the end of the graveyard shift.
If [i] can only find the switch to turnout the night light.

"She said if [i] could just touch the hem of His garment,
[i] know that [i]'d be made whole right now"
from "Touch the Hem of His Garment"

Sam Cooke

Connections

Aboriginal words flung into the well-walked soil of man,
the sacred hem of some carpenter's garment touched…
Something from out there has lain eggs on my soul
redefining the dusty school book isms of my street corner
beliefs, erasing "I" from my overly adorned cheap
Christmas tree image.
Things in themselves are useless
(a steering column without a car)
(a car without someplace to be);
meaning is the color that gives our portrait dimension.
Flowers and bees need each other,
like words need writers as actions need heroes.
The inner circle of embryonic ideas divide and dissolve
into a mounting allegorical anthology where pieces
of wrought-iron hopes become completed puzzles.
We need plugs for our sockets;
androgynous animals can equate to endless possibilities.
Even Nature, an imprint of God, needs waste to survive.
Wind blowing sweeping my lungs,
rain falling washing my dirty piggish deeds.
Lightening is liberated electricity.
Love is the thread that crochets it all into useful fabric.
My will now knows how to bend its stiff knees to float like
smoke to a higher plane where Love is the central
government, the sleeping force hibernating in us all until
the summer of His touch awakens us like petals unfurling
to the Sun's kisses.
Our actions are sticks that we rub together
to ignite eternal energy as a current connecting
ice to stone to metal to plastic to conservation…
Did [i] remember to put the blue bin out on trash day?

Traces of Old Lovers

Blistered skin bubbling from acid relationships
burn the palms of hands still throbbing from
the last hot-stove love…
We remain walking billboards of
a generation of glutinous lovers
with swelled and bloated bellies of bitterness.

In your neon eyes [i]'m blinded
by the piercing glow of your leftover lover.
The sight of his massive missile crashing
upon your eroding Earth burns brightly
as a meteor streaking across your hollow universe.
Yet, [i] pull down my shades, and
my eyes scamper away like rodents so
you may not see the still wet visions of the last female
who was the tin receptacle of my liquid waste.
We are two sleepy sets of eyes that can only meet
tightly glued in the dark.

Upon your branded skin [i] can smell the dried salt
of the last conqueror to plant his flag into your furrow.
[i] smell the boots of your last jockey before [i] know you.
Yet, no amount of perfume can wash away
the nature of aerobics [i]'ve performed in
sheets stained with women used as discarded dish rags.

Layered like stained shag carpet over scuffed floors,
old lovers drape our skin like wallpapered acne.
Our faces are a collage of cantankerous companions.
Stale kisses are glued forever upon our callus cheeks.
Crusty hand prints etched into the cracked sides
of our faces.
Tear tracks create deep grooved ravines of vertical lines
that intersect with horizontal wrinkled emotions stamped
by regret upon our buckskin foreheads as permanent
headstones.

Ruefully, we snarl and show our oral daggers at each other,

biting and barking at the shadows of ghosts long gone.
The mocking memories of past partners pollute our minds,
clouding our daily decisions.
We are held immobile by the albatross of old lovers.
Our tongues have licked salt too long to taste sugar.
Our concaved bed weighted by more people than it can
hold, we sleep one eye open never seeing each other.

> "Earning money in a factory
> is infinitely more important than
> spending it in an opera house."
> from *Up from Slavery*
>
> Booker T. Washington

Your Money's Life

Born solid, puberty dissolves it into a liquid,
able to be poured into any container of your need.
In its shaky history, it's been a barometric institution,
the yeast for the rise and fall of regimes,
the pointing hands on the compass for exploration,
the curved, abundant, and bouncing booty that launched
more ships than Helen.
It's been the bartered bullets for weapons,
the sanctimonious scent for haunting dogs,
the knot of the noose for lynch ropes,
the precious stone platform for kings,
the patron of wholesale constitutions of countries,
and the cornerstone of churches.
It's been exchanging the fate of the world
since man coined civilization.

But this tool of colonial carpentry is
slave to the master and wench to lord.
You can finance the fall of empires
or fund the power of your oppressor
by sailing your seeds with faulty maps.
You can sow knowledge for a currency tree or
roll it up in top paper, exhaling it away.

As any child, it must be breast fed and potty trained
and when mature enough sent off to higher institutions
to multiply the offspring of its family tree,
then taking its place as a productive asset of society.
This is the covenant; this do in remembrance
of your healthcare, retirement, and political donation.
For its life will be lived,

even if in somebody else's profiting pockets.

If this child receives
no candlelight or parental pushes from you,
it will boomerang against you,
go out and join cults of conservatism,
endure a perverted puberty, rise up, and strike you down.
You have no one to blame but your ignorant gluttony,
that big junk bond filled belly that keeps you in a coma.
Parenting is a process.
(A slave and his money…)
A parent must be together to raise together children,
or look dumbfounded
when the chickens come home to evict you.

She Became My Soul...

In was on Sapphire's Eve when from grace [i] fell.
From the plump pain of hands fingering the strings of my
soul, though [i] could not carve the words to yell,
in the contracting crater of my embryonic mind, [i] knew,
like Job on my meadow mattress, it was not the end...

And on the osmosis of my own humanity reborn of
morning dew spirituality, an unwrapped present my body
did hold, and from my single-cell self...
she became my soul...

Even before the pyramids of my own sexuality,
hieroglyphics with jig-sawed colors of the two of us
were born 'cause photosynthesis depends more on the
penetration of His will, if honey be from flowers and bees,
then she be from me, as Mother Earth swelled to inhale and
hold while she became my soul...

From the fiery fertilization of His touch,
Father God shoots showers over Mother Earth
yielding the Pierian of my heart beneath the soil of my will;
did the flowers of a fresh me begin to bloom;
she became my soul...

In the blue barathea crevices of my mind
is where her image soaks.
For of me she has always been a primary number
of my software's program.
Dancing, she static clings to the rhythmic umbilical chord
of our burrowing beats that lead to the depths of Truth.
And in man's fatal fall from forever, she is the spring
for a heaping generation of swimming repenters.

When flashing white fangs come for her, he comes for me.
She has always been my name, and my name hers,
written on the walls of forever and spoken on Time's
tongue, for she is my soul.

...written for strong sistas such as you

Carved in chocolate eminence and marble integrity,
a beauty of geometric complications
of curves, circles, arcs, and lines,
rich rigid resilience, butter smooth spirit,
and creamy features,
pearl round, smolderingly skeptic, and daring eyes
pose the question of freedom to my manhood
as they are set against the regal breadth of your nostrils
flaring with the panther pride of sovereignty
above your full, pouting, demanding, pleading, beguiling
lips from which words of wisdom, pain, and sugar pour,
constructing a mellifluous symphony of lineage:
Earth woman, the windy spring season of our revolution.
And even in your kitty timid tremble, your power
will sprout like a mightily majestic pear tree
from which many generations of Janies will be nourished.
In all of your red, black, and green essence,
you embody the ankh.
The fire of your temperament flashes strokes
of leaping orange coupled with fresh baked blues that
soothe sad skin, warm the area just below the navel, and
impregnate vivid possibilities into my mind's movie reel,
raising a sluggish soul that has lain for too long
under the diabetic weight of sexism.
Your check-to-check survival fertilizes me to action as the
easy pendulum of your hips slows me to a daze, thanking
God, His wine making son, and yo' mama for you.
Your Lucille Clifton melons seem to hand there, dangling
from your waist as treasured icons themselves.
In your wet womanhood
[i] will drown in your damp righteousness.
You've painted the landscape of our lives with your
sundry shades, tricolor moods, and wood oak fortitude,
all glossed and sealed by midnight oil
with caramel honey poured slowly over your soul's stalk.
Yet, even unpolished you shine.
Whether washerwoman, midwife, or neon Nefertiti,
your browns and Blacks drip like sugar from cane,

mixed with a golden twinkle that saunters around
your glow that will burn years after you have gone.
Your royal voice, snapping and popping its commands,
cracking verbs against the air as they sprout into deeds,
or the tightrope steady, perfectly rounded vowels
that roll from the sweet factory of your throat
and circle my life with lamb's wool.
You are the seed to my roots,
my night navigator to the shores humanity.
Our union is traced to before the worm infected the apple,
so even your Big Mama blues lift my lifeless body.
You are the skeleton protecting the organs of our love.
Your wooly hair, bronze body, and miracle mouth
make it easy to believe in God.
You are the authentic antiquity
that reminds me who [i] am.
Thank you for baptizing me
in your bottomless Black universe,
where [i] am raised with the name of genesis on my thigh.
You are the ropes of Time that pull me through;
this poem is written for strong sistas such as you.

Fever for Yo' Love Tonight

A telephone ringing after midnight is a trope in itself.
The sound of your raspy waking "Hello,"
rings like the "Sweet Jesus" prayers from
the moanin' bench of my loins.
The rivers of me burn like spewing lava pulled by gravity
down the side of marble mountains.
[i] smell your moist pith in my fertile imagination
and long to be anointed in the depths of you.
The urgent, vibrating growl in the deep of my throat
sends tickling chills down your treasure trail.
[i]'m a straw house soaked in gasoline;
allow me to unroll the hose of my fire engine.

Unlock the metal bolts of your heart's door;
unchain the password to the combination of your mind.
Tonight is when your lust blooms with mine.
Like a savior [i]'m taking on your sins to sanctify you.
The feral scent of your feline sensibilities been calling me
to be baptized in your sea.

Tonight ain't the time for calculus or contemplation.
Sometimes algebraic theory needs plotted actualization.
Let me be the lighted pathway to your dark imagination,
making your fantasy a soaked realization.

Whatever your cake and ice cream dreams want,
my well-honed creativity is at your demand,
not your boa constrictor mind,
but let your tingling thighs command.
This is the boiling kettle we've both been waiting for
turn the key of Solomon and walk through Pandora's door.

[i] gots the fever for yo' love tonight.
Let me be surrounded by yo' rivers to my left and right.
This is a fever that Tylenol can't fight;
can salvation be squeezed from your vice grips tonight?

Lush lands remain unexplored in the back of your mind;

let me rub your lamp, and your genie [i]'m sure we'll find
that an ox's desire to be free is not as strong as mine.
There must be fire if [i] smell your smoke all the time.

[i]'m burning like Yellowstone in July,
the notion that a fire will eventually burn itself out is a lie.
We have the opportunity to set
Cleopatra and Mark Anthony's tale right,
let my sugar cane sweeten your prosaic nights.

[i] gots the fever for yo' love tonight.
Odysseus would be proud to drown in yo' love tonight.
This is a foe dat even Achilles can't fight;
Helen knows that ravished and saved are the same tonight.

It's been Akhenaton's Aton since
[i] held you in my aching arms drank your raspberry rivers,
swam your sweet springs all night long.
My body is the tide to your moon.
This dam will explode
if [i]'m not allowed into your secret room.

[i] wanna connect the dots on you here and there,
give mouth to mouth to your lower lips
while tracing the myriad strands of each running hair.
Crashing myself against you,
let's find out if an ocean can be consumed by two.

You've taken all the space in my hardrive.
[i] need to download this overload.
Let me pry open the sealed gates to your flood.
The winds of our hurricane blow our ship from lust to love.

[i] gots the fever for yo' love tonight.
Let me spin you 'round in our carousel chambers tonight.
You are the "u" in my "lust" tonight.
Let's see if we can make the darkest night neon bright.
[i] gots the fever for yo' love tonight.

A Matter of the Dissolution of the Ghetto

Little Tina was never taught that Sex
is a separate monster from Cinderella's Love.
It gorges like a Celtic and sucks like a vacuum,
clawing the pearly hope from chaste children.
Pretty Tony's manhood was hung in his pants.
It's a one-eyed ego, a rugged cross, upon which
society hangs its antiquated anxieties.
Neither given many pebbles in their hourglass,
two more young throw-aways
raised by straight-razor streets.
The whole group wades the murky pool of unanswered
cries, acid tears burn, leaving scabs of social scars.
The whole group is dying,
decaying like fallen fruit from the inside.
Municipal Maggots eating their souls in circular motion,
leaving the city's inners
populated with partially digested shells.
Tina learned of affection through
the phlegm eyes of juvenile adults, rented kisses and
leased touches that excavate her inner regions
without the compassion of recycling,
leaving her soil stripped bare.
Pretty Tony was given the wrong *Webster*
which defined affection
as buying her something to eat before penetration.
Sun-time, both sentenced to a holding tank fenced by
grown folks who are waiting on
three o'clock and the thirtieth of the month.
Moon-time, babysat by slick suited pornography
and nasty nursery rhymes over Swahili beats.
Children are parenting children who are pirated by adults.
Tina's puberty parade begins,
and everyone shows up except her mama,
leaving a bearded boy as her Grand Marshall.
And Pretty Tony is a man because the police tell him so.
They, lost like Columbus, navigate backward waters,
taking discarded trash as triumphant treasures.
Algebra, American History, and Biology

do not reason with the reality of paying the rent.
Empty education houses push sterile curriculums.
Little girls play with Barbie Dolls
that require two a.m. feedings
as little boys have lemonade stands that sell rock candy.
Love and compassion are replaced by orgasms and weed.
In a swirling tornado moment,
two blind mice seek self gratification
to escape Now's rotting core;
backseat conception takes place.
Tina the Virgin is now Tina the Magdalene, and
Tony's toothless job has no healthcare plan.
Fourteen and fifteen year olds are the P in the PTA.
Sightless children led by myopic parents.
Another infant born to juveniles
who were raised by adolescents
who can't find the city of adults
for being astigmatic 'cause all the grandparents working the
three to eleven shift.
Ain't nobody grown at home.
A cycle of butchered butterflies birthed from moldy
cocoons, a game of suicide trying to out do manslaughter.
America digests its young, spoon feeding the world its
waste, and the ghetto is both farm and dump.

The Evil of Integration

All hail the Shimmering Sunrise of Supremacy.
Judge Lynch's Reform has come.
Congress' 104th has reversed the rivers of civil rights
on the scarlet whelped backs of its three-fifth citizens.
It's a roll call of plantation profiteers who
proudly pose before the Colonies
and chisel in blood the foundation of their pasty empire,
their contract on run-away urbanites
who believed themselves emancipated but failed to read
the fine print of the Freedom Finance Proclamation.

The Gingrich of Deceit is taking names.
The knives in his gore stained mouth water
and flash out for the blood of roasted dark meat.
The Dole of Classism dawns his ivory hood of hatred,
allowing only his bleeding eyes to expose the terror of
his soul as his words pretzelize the meshed mind's
of the masses upon demselves
making them a bucket full of crawfish.
Won't be long before the red rebel call of Duke is played.
It's all one Klan of a family.

And [i], [i] who believed the Disney ending of the 60s
am now forced to choke on the dry porridge of integration.

It's the evil of pale superintendents,
reigning down their plastic education
and molesting the hollow minds of red-bellied Ebony
babies with eyes that lead to condemned rooms
from being fed a constant diet of self-hatred
from an expired and contaminated can of Europe.
A drowning generation, reaching out at swords,
striking flesh wounds, bleeding, as a turtle, to death.
It's the Ghost of Segregation Past, lurking
in the distilled images of Ward, June, Ozzie, and Harriet,
touching his cold hands upon their trembling bodies,
keeping the NRA in business.
Yet, the smell of spilled blood,

decayed brains, and spoiled hopelessness doesn't perfume
the mayonnaise and cucumber air of their neighborhoods.

But this is the Age of Integration?

Where is my superintendent savior?
Where is my powerful principal?
They're all backseat assistants, castrated and
made impotent by the stainless steel knife of state funding.
Now "Step and Fetch It" are replaced by Watts and Franks,
the neo-house boys in office suits
doing the dirty dancing for the masters,
rounding up their people as recycled chattel for the 104th.

The good King Federick Govertgood has given way
to the Prince, Sir Satan Statehood,
as he picks his fangs clean, wiping the guts
of inner city delicacies from his cracked lips
as Jim Crow, the patient vampire, waits for his own return,
noose in hand, ashen to the bone.

It's not the silk white of Love or serenity.
It's the pale, chalky white of Death.
And Black becomes the color of suckers
who gave it all up to ride the front of the bus.
Mine eyes, burning with regret, have seen the coming of
the perverted progeny of integration.
His name be Clarence, and he defecates on the legacy
of the Trinity Amendments,
wiping his ass on the robe of Thurgood
while sitting atop the inferno toilet of inner cities,
hand feeding groundlings to Buchanan the Butcher
as they all say their prayers to Saint Ray-Gun,
giving his message to Columbus' new army
as it emanates through the Burnin' Bush.
It's the Klandestine Century of Tribulation.
But, this is integration?

Integration is an androgynous whore with two tongues.
She kissed us on our foreheads and sent us to sleep

with visions of a rainbow hued promise land
all the while seducing us out of our rights
with Cadillacs and the opportunity to marry ourselves white
or check other on the devil's demography form.
As we lay like dumbfounded concubines
fornicated by twelve years of Ray-Gunomics
that trickled down ass whippin's which
propelled us back to Big Missy's Kitchen.
Then we hear the alarm,
waking us to a snow white reality—
the sound of night sticks ringing out their revolution
on top of brother's back.

Burn Dream Burn.
This is the prize for what we were fighting,
giving us the opportunity to become Cadillac driving slaves
as Sir Clarence melts, [i] mean, integrates us all.

Vote!

A voting lever is the phallus of the people
that allows them to pollinate social policy.
So, if you don't vote, your words are soggy excrement
'cause a person who won't vote is like a man
who doesn't know what to do with his dick.
One by one we've got to impregnate this system
with the sperm of our philosophy.
If you don't want to be no new-packaged eunuch
allowing the people's history and hope the wither,
you'd better get off your rotting apathy and vote.

Having a big Johnson gets their attention,
but if you keep it your pants they won't do nothing.
In '92 we bent over in a position of submission,
and got stuck by the long stroke of the Fordice tradition.
Voting is society's way to employ and fire.
When your numbers swell to full length,
the candidates' résumés become saturated
with the swarming seeds of your agenda.
Having a big bat gets you in the game,
but if you don't swing it you can never get a hit.
Before 1965 all we could do is watch the game,
Now that we can play,
too many are choosing to sit in the stands.
Pulling a level is akin to pulling a trigger;
but just like Bigger we've often killed the wrong target.

From cargo in the bottom of boats to
flashing neon Negrolectuals with a vote,
voting is your fingerprint—
the data that documents your due diligence.
Not to vote is civil castration.
You might as well slit your wrist.
In this *Fortune* 500 we do have much stock.
Pulling the level allows us to commandeer
the national corporation block by block.
The history of Black bloody hopes is what you tote,
and you spill ethereal drops every time you refuse to vote.

A Bullet for the Drug Dealer

[i] wish that the last sociable sound that rings in your ears is
the explosion of a single round colliding sledge hammer
style with the side of your skull, sending fragments of bone
and brain flying defiantly about the air as ants ridding
themselves of a poisoned mound.

The thump of your rag doll body
against the uncaring concrete,
the urban purgatory, no music could ever sound that sweet.
[i] wonder if upon contact with air would little dancing
demons come crawling, spider-like, from your blood.
They'd probably flash gang signs to the nearest camera,
so [i]'d shoot their little asses too.

They say you can't kill the devil.
But, [i] know that you are not he; you don't have the pull to
park on Pennsylvania Avenue.
You are just a second-hand, remote controlled Trojan
Horse attacking Black villages worst than HIV.

In my sleep your face is a smashed silver can, scratched
and dented by kids kicking you constantly down the
concrete street. Your smile a wolfen snarl,
saliva dripping between each grunt.
In your gutted growl [i] hear the shrieking cries of children
lost to you, their lives food for your machine.
Your veins drip poison, IVs for your clients.
We are a caged community attached
by the shackles of dope,
a dirt-colored human circle of spoiled egg death.

But my boiling bullet for you
begins in the basement of my soul.
To think of killing is to mold like forgotten cheese.
[i] go, crumb by wilting crumb, as erosion,
with every cyanide thought of your deliberate death,
until we are both empty frames or abandoned houses;
transparent and identical, [i] pull the trigger.

Black In...

Guitar strings pulled back,
releasing screams that stab the night.
[i] just wanna know
(Is there another face in the painted sky)?
'Cause [i] just wanna show that
(only Truth can walk naked and untouched
through a room full of molesters.)
                  So dig!
Back Black a Nile River time ago
when the pale ones didn't know (how to take the Funk),
tried to fake the Funk,
colonize the Funk,
just to be near the Funk,
even tried to fornicate the Funk,
never realizing that all of the colors like patterns on a quilt
are stitched and surged by the Funk.
The thunder of its voice was calling my name.
This freak-a-fantastic fame
which middle c did proclaim
the orientation of colors—
finding that Truth in any color is always Black...
even anti-colored anthropologists will tell you so.

Well Black on, Brother Black, Black on...Thus,

the Black in the night is the bright in the light of white.
(Can you dig?) [i] yam what [i] yam
'cause [i] likes sweat potatoes with butter.
So-----shake your paintbrushes. Evolution's calling!
Put on your sunglasses and bathe
in the sauna of bright Black.

As Stevie did wonder ten million lives ago (do you know)
how many building blocks your body has?
Yo' mind and yo' spirit are the batteries to your ass.
Tap, like a made-to-order hydrant, into the power of color,
funky faucets be pouring out liquid that we needs,
causing crayolas to come together to create worlds.

Strokes of Black twirl inwardly drinking,
discharging colors on the way down,
collapsing into technicolor hues of
sundry seasons, tie-dye cities, and mauve moments.
So you better grab a roller and let your colors flow freely.

Pull all of the colors from the womb of Black
and smell the licorice of the night
speckled with bits of strawberry dust.
Take a lick of the apple-licious atmosphere.
Colors exploding like an overdue pregnancy
framed in the shimmering lines of
Black satin sheets draped over the Sun.
Rays of ebony gold sprinkle powdered sugar
into the awaiting mouths of your future.
God is the Funky Painter,
the human race His hieroglyphics,
the linguistic rainbow of His personal mosaic.

Funk is the air of our lungs.
Funk is the sway of our walk.
Funk is the melody of our booty.
Funk is the dip in our dap.
Funk is the hymn of our hearts.

Somebody brangs me a mirror so [i] can looks at my Funk.

      Turn out the lights so that you can see better. Your soul has eyes that you've never used. It never needs sunshades. Calm the raging reds, greens, and blues and float out into a sea of paintashia. Feel the rayon hues blowing upon your emotions. You are a rocket ship shooting, Black raspberry of a race. Forever in His collage you are kept safe. Don't let nobody take your paintbrush from you. Peace and Goodnight.

...speaking from masculine to feminine

My masculine wants to speak to you.
My male wants to speak to your female.
It's the primal urges of the mating season,
and the air is sodden with your pheromone.
It smells wet and pink upon my nose.
A moist residue is left upon my face.
It tastes like your sweet potato image,
a buttercup soul dipped in chocolate cake batter.
May [i] lick the bowl?
[i] sense your coy beauty in the
hide and seek games you play:
your words set in stone,
chiseled by hands of expert experience,
your inner magnet, the positive to my negative,
making me digest the feminine.
Angry, feline squinted eyes,
crossed from reading an anthology of lies,
roll across the unedited sky, searching
for the cliff notes to their pain.
Purposely misused words that linger like perfume,
hoping to flush out the kinks of my true aspirations.
Faintly, they fall to the floor like pieces of glass.
Your ability to stay right even when left of correct,
clenching your fist,
your female credo to stab or caress me.
Your beauty seems to be rooted
as an ancient tree in an abyss seen only by eyes
that last saw the leaf of the first tree.
Your soul is a raven butterfly which,
when inverted, explodes infinite colors,
which converge into endless emotions of Charity.
As a male it vibrates like new Pioneer speakers to me.
[i] want to deduce the unsolvable equation that is you.
My masculine to your feminine.
Is that fear [i] smell, bubbling cinnamon cut with cherries;
or is it the bitter lemon of uncertainty's honesty?
Your trembles against the night air, each movement
jerking and pulling your center into a climactic contusion.

These are the things that we hide
under our gray and brown attire,
locked down by our leashes,
belts and shoe strings all knotted too tightly,
leaving fuchsia tinted marks and whelps that
burn at various angles across our bodies.
Nightly, we lick our wounds,
unashamed of being male and female.
At dawn, we burrow out of our holes
to face another day as upright animals.
Only the cloaked smell follows us,
sending overdue notices to our pleading psyches.
[i] am immersed in the salty smell of your shame,
held captive in your maze of human boxes,
longing to study the index and glossary of your anatomy
for the empirical always trumps the abstract.
[i] believe in the deity of woman.
Curves of wisdom and mountains of kindness,
[i] am conquered by your puissance.

Corner-Stone

Mrs. Ruth McInnis
Born into this life: August 12, 1916
Born into Eternity: December 1, 1993

The corner-stone of the family,
the root of a mighty tree,
a cable-locking, reinforcing foundation
for your duckling seeds, your apples and oranges.
Upon your stainless steel faith and pit-bull devotion
you are the orchard from which springs a forest of heritage,
cultivating your family with
charity's chicken soup in your heart
and the torah's swift sword in you hands,
as you worked like a planter, tilling and pruning the weeds
of evil from your garden, raising your child crops in
the succulent shadow of love
pointing them to the eternal lamp post,
flowing like fruitful spring rivers.
With the balm of your words, you soothed our bodies
when they ached of deferred dreams.
You spared not the reckoning rod
when we were waywardly wondering sheep.
You calmed our firehouse anger with your lullaby looks.
And, you wiped away our raining eyes
when we were woeful from the world's wrongs.
What cast iron sculptures you and Rob have welded,
no visionless man can put asunder.
This foundation was built on cornbread and covenant.
And on each page of your life,
you allowed God to edit and perfect bind
under the umbrella of His Love.
We are truly the house that Rob and Ruth built.
And upon that parental platform
shall we stand redwood tall and
multiply this genesis of goodness because
you allowed it to be molded
according to God's paradigm.
In us are your seeds of love

because love is the only currency you had,
sending us to bed under the quilted lives
of ancestors gone on before us.
This is why in God's plush comforter
we are now able to abide.
Like a lamb on the cross,
to your family you gave your life,
just as to Rob, God gave a wife.
And the monsoon of blessings
affirms for us that He is pleased.
You made for Him a family
four generations fold.
In our hearts, field peas and front porch memories
along with oak wood truth are forever etched in gold.
We are your Gibraltar and Stonehenge
that will forever stand time.
So we will always hear from heaven
the crystal ringing of your chime.
Though you are a permanent stitch in our blood's fabric,
Now you belong to the ageless quilts of heaven.
Thank you, we bathe in your love forever.

Mother of Illegitimates

Snatched intervals of joyous numbness
like remnants of dusk giving way to dawn
are the moments of her bliss as little ones
await her return like lost puppies.

Bidding farewell is her only constant,
quicksanding her way through motherhood
with quick flashes of dull heat waves.
She is limp prey between two predators,
motherhood rages and crashes its
flesh stained claws against
the blood soaked fangs of romance.

Boomeranging to love her kids,
dying in the crucifixion of romance,
she'll be right back in three days,
her soul wears a life that's two sizes too small,
sleep be her only comfort.
Circular demands spin her drunk.
No one collects and saves her tears;
she's crushed between the
demands of little people and womb-less women.
Her self is hollowed out,
filling her shell with the guts of others.
Emotionally bloated and mentally constipated,
she's waiting for the ice cream call
of death's voice
to usher her home…

The Ramblings of a Scarred Mind

Okay, but only if honesty strokes you into ecstasy
since you are as compelled (as falling leaves are
to find the ground) by your fear
with its frosty fingers on the small of your security
pushing you to face the eviscerated hells of your dreams
that my sanity is a thumbnail to yours.

On days that outnumber my counting,
my hands burn from the ropes of sanity
slipping through my weakening grasp, greased
by the person who thinks it funny to move
my chair two inches to the left everyday.
The saline sweat from my crumpled brow
seeps into my pin pierced eyes, sizzles, and returns
with tears from the bowels of my spoiled memory,
twisted and disfigured, a wrinkled case with soft inners.
My sanity is worn away like over tilled farm soil.

"…and a good day to you, sir…"
a return echo spoken to ghosts of lost yesterdays

The heavy weight of the focus of your eyeballs on my face
leaves tiny indentations that [i] finger incessantly.
The clanking noise of your thoughts
pounds against the tin walls of my mind.
Shut up damit!...(Did [i] say that out loud?)
My carnival fears are afraid of themselves.
Their stares poke me like a cattle prod.
[i] can feel the teeth of your opinions
picking away, peeling my insides from each other.
The ashy hand of your distain runs along my
inner chest cage as the joints of your fingers
work to squeeze my life in your python palms.

Am [i] your looking glass?
Can you drink if my waters are dammed?
Whose salvation is in the pot of this poker game?
Go ahead, run. The doors of the church are open.

God is sitting atop His erect mountain.
Is it the mountain that makes Him the almighty
with His "I know a secret" smile?
Is He smiling His glowing graces down on me?
Or, is He smiling at His soon to be extinct creature?
Fuck it; He made me. His smile is a sermon.
"Love is water that rejects your oil. Your flesh is
sown from the waste of this world that I
will cast off and leave behind when my day comes."
Isn't everyday His day, and if it isn't
aren't we living a lie?
[i] experience *Lost Paradise* on a daily basis.
[i] curse. He smiles.
[i] kneel before Him. He smiles.
My lump of coal body collapses beneath the
foot of his merry mountain;
rocks and pebbles scratch their nails
into my spine. He smiles.

This is your God.
My faded memories of Sunday school are all that [i] have,
and therein lies our parting waters.

Of Reality and Perception

Perception has Reality in a Radio Flyer wagon,
pushing and pulling it to points along a course
where a series of arbitrary events become
some well-paid historian's revolution.

All things having weight, occupying space,
existing in altered states of being in my mind's microscope
are gathered together for future use.
(If [i] can just remember where [i] put them all.)
Memory is the Matrix that produces Reality.
How my mind's eye can sculpt reminiscence
of what [i] smell to protect against repeating mistakes.
(She's wearing the same perfume as my ex-wife.)
How sound manifests itself as a memorial
etched forever in my mind, puppeteering my next move.
(That chick is tweeting the same sorrowful song.)

Perception is the coordinates on the graph to Reality.
How they are plotted within this equation depends on your
understanding of the math accessible to you.
(I didn't know that she was married.)
(The money was just lying in the street when [i] got there.)
Perception is the overcoat worn by Reality;
or, is it Reality's internal organs.
Reality waits like clay for the molding hands of Perception.

Reality is conceived when
Perception has intercourse with History.
Memory, like choosing lovers, is subjectively selective.
[i] vaguely remember what happened,
depending on the ramifications of the happening.
And the "now" is created from pieces of the past
that [i] keep in my pocket to figure out what it tastes like.
Life is the ever constant flow of this sewage.
[i] hope that you have a good plunger.

StarGazer

StarGazer sits on his mountain top,
his Black chiseled body
cloaked in a silver, silk garment
the moonlight radiating off his
Alkebu-Lan deus body
(ebon and pearl swirl in an onyx stone).
His thoughts of the night beam outwardly,
his gazing across the universe, allowing his body
to soak in the still waters of the night.
His soul's secret sanctuary flashes and flickers
like the rayon fires of scented candles
against the dark recesses of our murky minds.
His rainbow emotions cascade down his spine like
rain down a marble mountainside,
washing away the painful dirt of our day.
Slightly shivering from a slow breeze, female in its touch,
he lays his intense thighs and calves upon the grass top,
extending horizontally his sleek back to touch
east and west, so that every muscle feels
the limber liberation from stoic stiffness.
His flecked coffee eyes pierce through the raven sky
into the depths of God's almshouse.
It's so bright, Black, and beautiful,
covered with the champagne of ebony gold.
And God returns his intense, earnest look with
a smile and a tear that gently drops from Heaven
rolling down the side of the universe,
and upon the artifact of the StarGazer.
He is re-baptized in possibility, anointed with a strength
that allows his eyes to never defy the stars.
They are the soil to his root, receiving their energy through
the pores of his skin, the receptors of their emotions.
As the night plays a concerto,
the stars dance over his frame.
He, the good shepherd, watches them,
keeper and protector of the stars.

Is There a Difference Between Purple and Grape?

The contrived complexity of color is
as American as colonization and apple pie.
Rights and Wrongs are Siamese hybrids of the (T)ruth.
Black and White exist in the Lego dimensions of need.
Certainties exist in the monetary liquidations
of emotions for units of time.
[i] guess it's political what truths with which we sleep.
Even the eyes of my soul are unable
to focus the vibrating barometer between
social awareness and political agenda.
It's much like the relation of purple to grape
or even their plummet in the fashion polls to lavender.

[i] mean, is cream a dirty white?
Or, is tan a mulatto brown?
All my human boxes clutter my attic
where my naiveté is pimped
and turned into a pious platform,
yet my sanity is based on
simplification, deception, and ideological assimilation.
Purple is a crayon, grape is a fruit drink,
 and lavender is the curtains my wife bought.

What's scary is that [i] understand
the understood difference.
Yet, [i] still don't know if cream is dirty,
and if using political Purex constitutes selling out.
What parties have to be crossed before color changes,
before midnight Black is pearl Black,
or "Thurgood" Black is "Clarence" Black,
especially with the confusion of fabric and hue?
Most of my outfits are mixed matched.
There are no purely indigenous colors.
All Americans are mongrels, mutts if you prefer.

Time

Moving, in its own oiled engine, flinging our floppy bodies
from the bumps of its meandering train ride with an open-
ended ticket of no expiration date.
Still, the ultimate cleaner of our bathroom lives.
Peering at us over the rim of its pearl Black bifocals, its
leopard smile drips with the delight of our tender mortality.

Time's reality exists in a brick solid state of now.
Our lives televised reruns of continuous allusions, which
we desperately try to knit and stitch together with worn and
tattered representations of thrown away clichés.
And when Time's roach stomping size twelves trample our
precisely placed plastic Barbie Doll houses, our lives flat
line into a constant current of redundant allegory.
We are consumed by the horizontal span where the sky
touches the ground and our youth surrenders to age as our
dreams are eaten by bacteria of daily disappointment.
Time, like swarming enzymes, deconstructs our inners,
dismantling termite style the human being
wherein Time becomes its own beehive, its own bungalow,
relegating History as window dressing to our memories.

Its John Henry bulging arms
brush against our straw-hut lives.
In its bottomless eyes we fall forever,
never catching us but bouncing us from hand to hand.
And often, we see the twinkle in its left eye,
take false comfort; brief flashes, blinded, and we awake
wrinkled, grayed, slowed, and desperate.
It's straightedge mouth haunts us.
We build cosmetic walls to keep it out, or is it to keep it in?
We meticulously measure it, but its sand still slips away.
We break it, like bread, in half, naming it night and day,
and we still don't know when to sleep.
We carve it like a pie, and its calories kill us.
It laughs at us, mockingly presenting its tonsils,
the vibration causing us to spring forward and fall back.
So we lie to ourselves and reset the Sun's clock.

We name its days, weeks, months, and years,
but have no clue what time it is.
Our artificial beliefs eventually crumble
as man-made empires into the sea.
And if it doesn't get you in the wash,
it will surely get you in the rinse;
for putting the Sun in a watch will eventually cause you to
slit your wrist, signifying the meaningless nothing of our
lives elevated by us, the clock watchers.

In Time, the reveled secret under the community cloth is
that the synthetic garden grown essence of our paintings
of Time by which we drum our being is as fake as
canned vegetables and self-cleaning ovens as we attempt
to cut the circle in two to find our alpha and omega.
Yet we find there is no finish line to this marathon,
no final stop on our greyhound, only flowing Time, no
greater or lesser, no superior or inferior.
Our measurements are the vain actions
of wearing a girdle to sleep.
There is only Time and us;
we are ants crawling across a deserted desert.

It surrounds but never touches us
like an angry mob taunting a leper.
It's a swinging door continuing to open and close on our
lives, tempting us to action, scaring us to inaction.
It is the liquid ability of language,
flowing toward no specific ocean.
The eyes of Time are blind to us.
Its motive is to merely be a canvas.
It eats when it's not hungry, or is it History's tapeworm.

And if [i] find abysmal beauty in its deadbeat fathering of
us, in its eternal yet aloof omnipresence,
and through my meek morality,
it's because [i] am able to see from being brushed
by Time's brilliantly sublime hands.

Another Trip on the Eve of Insanity

Murky water children with your ragged baggage of
burdens, we're all being flushed away.
There's a time boom ticking within the depths of
the rotted cavity where souls used to be, and
our ears are jammed full of cotton fear.
We'd all rather stay in the playground of fiction
with the slimy workings of a sexual serpentines,
mentally masturbating away our anxieties.

Father Mercy, can you slip some spiritual smelling salt
into the nose of my sleepy soul before it's too late?

Street corner children cry cloudbursts of sorrow
deep into the charcoal pit of the night.
The sweltering rays of our anger shine
a fool's gold illusion of ourselves
where the porch light is confused with the moon.
We fall on Saint Adam's eve,
heeding the call of a mutated morality
where pain is the pleasure of orgasm.

Father Mercy, can you slip some spiritual smelling salt
into the nose of my sleepy soul before it's too late?

A-pop-call-us goes my mind to an apocalypse rhyme
over a dirty road beat that's accompanied by
an un-tuned piano that sounds of drowning kitties
suffocated in broken bagpipes.
Yet the original Prince of Music
seduces me to join his choir.
If all is yours, why are you so far away from you?
Father Mercy, can you slip some spiritual smelling salt
into the nose of my sleepy soul before it's too late?

As curled up possums, we lie on our stiff board backs
afraid to vacation from consciousness
for fear of being ravaged by the creeping things of our
mind, but never sane enough to fear insanity.

Father Mercy, can you slip some spiritual smelling salt
into the nose of my sleepy soul before it's too late?

Now [i] lay me down to slumber, praying the devil's
spyware doesn't have my soul's social security number.
If [i] die before [i] wake,
[i] wonder which of my souls the Lord will take.
Insanity's white suited agent
attempts to make a deal for my waived intellect.
No longer a member of my body's ball club,
it wanders the streets looking for a critic to stroke it.
Yet, [i] am told by a nameless purple soothsayer
to hold on to the value of my soul for there is a better way
to play hopscotch than in the middle of the highway.
The wretched winds of reality cut through my body,
playing a torpid stillborn melody against my bones.
A cup of something offers to warm me, drowning my
frozen hatred and arctic sadness with the blistering bite of
bootlegged illusion; [i] am sustained by my Everclear lies.

Father Mercy, can you slip some spiritual smelling salt
into the nose of my sleepy soul before it's too late?

Silent Conscience

An explosion of soiled and spoiled spirits
ring rusted lullabies, a carbonated crying conscience
held silent by contentment.
Bankrupt and sterile tears plunging to the ground
within the depths of our barren being.
A screaming mother's pleas
crash against the ashy quarry of the night.
Her baby's lying in a milky lagoon of blood,
and [i] toss and turn in my rundown crib
while the wobbly world with its skewed axis,
just keeps turning, ignoring its irregular humming.
We need spiritual q-tips to hear conscience set on silent;
it's the unwavering voice of high-pitched sorrow
asking us to reread the fine print of *Walker's Appeal*
to the *King James Pamphlet* on our mind's nightstand.
The roosters of evil have a first-class ticket
back to the coop.
Can't you hear it tapping you on your soul's eardrum?
But the flesh is anesthetized,
paralyzing our spirits to a hollow shell.

Silent Conscience sings a serene song
under the noise of clanging cash registers
as there is yet another white sale.

The heated name of Jesus (the original bronze brother)
rings like a national weather alarm and falls on frozen ears.
Yet, it's still steamrolling the tracks of our minds,
bouncing off the brick and wrought iron walls
of our apathy, fighting for position
because evil keeps a constant hard-on.
If we don't get a condom for our souls,
we'll become pregnant with the bastard seeds
of Satan's loins, and there ain't no DHS for demons.

Silent Conscience whispers as a nation's narcolepsy
holds it under the winter blankets of immorality
as the world just keeps spinning its mud stuck wheels.

A man with a sign, "Will work for food,"
stands beneath a sign, "50 billion served."
This *object d'art* is framed in finely finished avarice.
Still we do not hear it creeping like dust mites
down our rickety spines, lurking in our minds like lice.
Our nature is past its expiration date.
The spirit can't grow when the body lies in an impure bed.
Still it calls, moaning like a siren, howling like a wolf
with a frozen winter's trap gnawing away its paw,
flashing his teeth across our dreams.

If we don't hear the howling horrors of
Tuskegee, Money, Philadelphia, the Congo, or Rwanda,
how can we hear what haunts Pearl or Littleton?

Silent Conscience knocks at the door of our brain;
however, opportunity has started the car to leave.

Children of Trouble

Trouble's children dining on the entrée of
decayed dreams, facing their flowering age
during the vandalism of their minds,
people backhanded with the backlash of their rotten seeds.
We are the boars of intellectualism
grounded like minced meat in mercantilism's machine.
We've got to sanitize our souls instead of smothering them
in a lumpy religion with a mummifying hold.
Desperately drowning people in the cesspool of capitalism
reaching for salvation, finding flawed flotation devices
poked full of holes to save on overhead.
Laughing children with plastic smiles of insanity,
crying children soaked with reality's
lemon bitter and salty tears, never realizing
that what they lost wasn't worth having.

Bastards of society searching for the roots of their fallen
tree, branching out without direction, never growing
only devolving into shells of shadows.
The age of reason is devoid of logic.
Justification allows sleep to serve as a proper religion.
Ours is the want of a heaping serving or more nothing
with a side of spicy nihility.
Iron souls move along to a rhythm absent of groove,
clanging loudly with a bridge that leads to nowhere.
Paper hearts filled with the hollowed rhetoric of the times
that turns on them like termites when thinking is beckoned.
Frantic fanatics on fire for Jehovah's finances,
call upon God to do their dirty work,
to keep their hands free for salvation.

Pop Poetry

It's the mystery of the lost sock to me the way most poets
attempt to create poems sautéed with history
so that their names will be written
in *Norton's Book of Eternity*.
An anthology is just the next mockingbird's opinion.
And you'll never go to the dance,
waiting to be invited by the embalmed old dominion.

[i] don't give a damn 'bout my work's hereafter;
the right now culture is what my words are after.
Hitting the moment's bull's eye is all that matters.
Readership tomorrow won't pay my spiritual bills.
Soul-less scholars revering me don't give me no thrills.

[i]'m not trying to fade my polka dot blazer
into a spineless style that blends.
And [i]'m not trying to be falsely framed and published
by my patron beholding friends.
Nor is it about whether or not my work sells,
[i] don't spend sleepless nights
wondering if my ship will sink or sail.

Compete with the formal lie of
Chaucer, Shakespeare, and Milton
and get your ass whipped by the psychedelic children.
Go ahead and write your odes
to thangs that don't happen anymore,
and the only response you'll get is a resounding snore.

You can trip and pay these pop icon's no mind,
and when its time to move the leftover people,
you'll be left on your crusty and brittle behind.
That impotent, academic artist gig is tired.
[i] don't know any relevant artists who are retired.
So, go ahead and be summarily scholarly.
[i] just plan to make a little noise with my pop poetry.

Dear Reader:

    With my tongue in your mouth and my beating organ in your hand, [i] can be a paroled man, and you'll always know where [i] stand. Dig? [i] can only hope that these expressions created at least tiny explosions in your thinking space. These are simply the orgasms of my soul, climaxing off the experience of moments bookmarked by the rise and fall of the Sun. You just got to take time to play with it.

                              Peace, rain, and sunshine…
                              Rainbows forever,
                              C. Liegh McInnis

p.s.

Always turn it around and look at it from the back…

www.ingramcontent.com/pod-product-compliance
Lightning Source LLC
Chambersburg PA
CBHW032213040426
42449CB00005B/582